Pablo Escobar:

The True Story Of The Worlds Most Famous Drug lord

By Luke Johnson

Thank you for purchasing Pablo Escobar:
The Worlds Most Famous Drug Lord.
This book follows the story of infamous drug baron
Pablo Escobar and the Medellin Cartel. Information
sourced from various sources attempt to give a
multidimensional and unique look into the life and
violence that surrounded and was left in the wake
of Pablo Escobar.

This document is geared towards providing exact and reliable information in regards to the topic and issue covered. The publication is sold with the idea that the publisher is not required to render accounting, officially permitted, or otherwise, qualified services. If advice is necessary, legal or professional, a practiced individual in the profession should be ordered.

- From a Declaration of Principles which was accepted and approved equally by a Committee of the American Bar Association and a Committee of Publishers and Associations.

In no way is it legal to reproduce, duplicate, or transmit any part of this document in either electronic means or in printed format. Recording of

The information herein is offered for informational purposes solely, and is universal as so. The presentation of the information is without contract or any type of guarantee assurance.

The trademarks that are used are without any consent, and the publication of the trademark is without permission or backing by the trademark owner. All trademarks and brands within this book are for clarifying purposes only and are the owned by the owners themselves, not affiliated with this document.

TABLE OF CONTENTS

Intro

During a period of excess, a street thug that became a billionaire feeding America's insatiable thirst for the manic energy of cocaine. The story of Pablo Escobar, is one of a middle class child, born during a violent civil war that went down a path of petty crime at an early age, but due to unfettered ambition, cunning intellect and inhuman violence became one of the most ruthless and successful drug lords in history. His empire grew to such a point that entire governments and innumerous resources were dedicated to his apprehension, it be dead or alive. In its essence though this is a story of death, mass murder and violence, all for the sake of luxury drugs and ravenous greed.

La Violencia

Pablo Escobar was born on the first of December in 1949, the third son of a school teacher and a farmer. The Escobar family had seven children in total. Their third son, Pablo had ambition that would be evident from a very young age, he was heard to frequently tell his friends that he intended on becoming the President of Columbia, when in actuality he would rather kill a presidential candidate than become one. In essence a cosmic precursor to Escobar's violent life, Pablo was born during a bloody ten year civil war, known simply as La Violencia, or *The Violence* in translation.

 La Violencia was sparked by the assassination of Liberal Party leader and presidential candidate Jorge Eliécer Gaitán, which resulted in a 10 hour riot with a death toll of five thousand people. Others speculate that the violence started as a result of

Conservative Party farmers being encouraged to forcibly take land from Liberal party supporting farmers. The total death toll of the entire conflict is estimated to be a staggering two hundred thousand people. The methods the guerrilla groups used to kill and intimidate were brutal and inhumane. Including the mass rape of young school girls, the indiscriminate killing of infants (some by bayonet), beheadings, crucifixion and more creative methods. It is said that they would remove fetuses from pregnant women by cutting into their womb and replacing the unborn child with a rooster. As testament to the repercussions of La Violencia on society, the preferred method of killing used by Columbian drug-dealers, the Columbian necktie, was invented during this period. This vicious method of killing involved the victim's throat being slit and then their tongue would be pulled down the throat and hung out the slit. La Violencia was the school that taught an entire generation of drug dealers how effective death, torture and intimidation where as tools to promote their interests. This could have possibly been the bloody incubator that created the Cartel leader, Pablo Escobar, which had little to no regard for human life and a sociopathic level of detachment for the pain of others.

The Yeyo

[Cocaine] It can create a powerful craving to use more cocaine. Repeated cocaine use leads to tolerance. -
WebMD

Cocaine affects the body in multiple ways, the most immediate and noticeable, is that it gives you the perception of limitless energy and a feeling of invincibility. It activates the pleasure centers of the brain, creating an immense feeling of euphoria, a heighten sense of cognitive awareness and focus. The problem is that due to the high price of cocaine, it is often "cut" or substances are added to increase its volume. If your lucky it will be baby formula or pulverized laxatives. If you're unlucky it can be cut with deworming medication which has the ability to shut down your immune system, borax (or boric acid) which is a cleaning agent, powered laundry detergent and local anesthetics to mimic the numbness cocaine causes. Most street level cocaine has a purity of around 20 to 30 percent. The high from cocaine is short lived which results in the user wanting more and over time the user can develop a tolerance which means they need more cocaine to get high. Eventually it creates a crippling addiction, as the user seeks the feeling of their first high (also called "chasing the dragon"). Cocaine is a product that sells itself and Pablo made billions selling it.

After studying for a very short time at Columbia's Universidad Autónoma Latinoamericana in Medellín, Escobar decided his road to wealth and power wouldn't involve following legitimate channels. With his very first collaborator, Oscar Aguirre, they started committing opportunistic street level crimes including selling counterfeit lottery tickets, cigarettes that were contraband and even stolen car parts. Eventually, motivated by Escobar's unbridled ambition, their criminal activity escalated with the kidnapping of a business executive, which he was paid $100.000 to release. Although sources seem to conflict regarding the timing, it was during this period that Pablo also started smuggling contraband cigarettes into Columbian at a larger scale. He soon became one of the key players of the so called "Marlboro Wars" a power struggle for the control of Colombia's supply of illegally imported cigarettes. Although he had dropped out of University this was the college that would teach him the ins and outs of moving illegal materials and controlling an illicit market. In 1975 Medellin Cartel member Fabio Restrepo was assassinated and although it was never confirmed it is widely suspected that Escobar pulled the trigger, or at least ordered the hit. Shortly after Escobar approached Restrepo's crew and according to reports, told them they would work for him now. This was the beginning of the man that would go down in history as the world's most prolific drug dealer.

From here Pablo started evolving into the juggernaut that gained him a solid place in the annuals of crime history.

Escobar through cunning business acumen and a unquenchable thirst for power and wealth started expanding Restopo's operation. He would import the coca paste from both Peru and Bolivia, initially even flying the airplanes loaded with coca paste himself between Panama and Colombia. His main source of the coca paste was Bolivia and Peru, he would then ship it into Colombia, process it and smuggle it into the United States. There were two times during this period that almost brought Pablo's operations to a halt. During one instance it is reported by Pablo's son, that his father was forced to preform an emergency landing resulting in the death of a close friend of Escobar. The crashed plane would later adorn the entrance to his drug empire's headquarters, La Hacienda Napoles. In retrospect, much like Hitler felt motivated to leave his mark on the world after a near death experience, this event might have been instrumental to Pablo's ascension. The second instance that almost ended Pablo's criminal career, was when he was arrested with a number of his associates after being caught with 18 kg of coca paste as they attempted to smuggle it into Colombia. Instead of ending him, much like the airplane crash that killed his friend, this experience also seemingly molded and formed the man that Escobar became. After unsuccessfully trying to bribe the judges that would be overseeing his drug possession case, he killed the policemen that had apprehended him, resulting in the case being thrown out, due to the lack of material witnesses. This became the model of business and negotiation Pablo became famous for, *Plomo o Plata,* Lead or Sliver. The authorities that would go up against him and his empire, had a choice to either be bought or die.

Roberto Escobar accountant of the Medellin Cartel and Pablo's brother has an interesting fact about

Pablo's decision to enter the drug business. According to Roberto the reason Pablo began drug smuggling and dealing was because it was safer and less competitive than contraband cigarettes and products. At the time of Pablo's first forays into drug smuggling there were no cartels and few drug lords, thus there was enough work for everyone without much of a threat due to competition. Beyond that, authorities and drug enforcement agencies were essentially oblivious to the threat of cocaine, instead concentrating their efforts on the drug of the day: marijuana. By today's standards this seems comically naïve on behalf of the government agencies. Of course this would soon change.

Roberto not only survived the decimation of the Medellin Cartel but actually still lives in Medellin and even wrote a book about his experience as the accountant of one of the world's biggest criminal empires. He says in his book that at the height of their activity, they would spend more than a thousand dollars a month just on rubber bands to wrap the staggering amounts of money they made from the sale and distribution of cocaine. Roberto is also the curator of a Pablo Escobar museum which is housed in the hide-out that he and Pablo used right before Pablo was killed. It still holds both Pablo's dirt bike and the blue truck he used when smuggling coca paste.

The very first source of the coca paste Pablo secured was in Peru and only managed to purchase 30 kg initially. During this first foray he would smuggle the coca paste into Medellin where it was cut and processed into cocaine powder in a small two story building. As demand grew for "California Cornflakes" so did Pablo's and the Medellin Cartel's operations.

Plata o Plomo

The eighties came and with it a huge financial boom which can be assumed was at least *partially* fuelled by Pablo's product. Disco was dead, South Beach was were everyone wanted to be and Wall Street bankers and brokers were practically royalty. It was a time of excess; excessive parties, excessive greed and excessive cocaine use. The expensive white power became the newest and hippest designer drug of the era. At this point in history the Medellin cartel was responsible for a whopping 80 to 89 percent of all the cocaine brought into the United States. This insatiable hunger for "Columbian Gold" would earn Pablo and the Cartel a mind blowing 420 million dollars *a week.*

Due to the increase in demand fueled by the neon clad 80s, Pablo enlisted the help of Carlo Lehder.

Lehder became Escobar's and the Cartel's logistics officer, moving the cocaine produced in Medellin to the United States through various smuggling routes. At one point to facilitate the movement of the drugs, Lehder bought the majority of Norman's Cay, a small island just under 400 km off the coast of Florida. This served as a mid-way point for the transportation of the vast amounts of cocaine and featured a home for Lehder, a hotel, an airstrip with a fleet of 15 airplanes and even a large refrigerated warehouse to store the Cartel's product. After buying the initial pieces of land, Lehder through strong arm and scare tactics managed to force the remaining inhabitants off the island. It not only became a depot for refueling and rest for the drug smugglers it was also Lehder's personal adult playground. According to one of Lehder's pilots, Carlos Toros, he was picked up at the island's airstrip in a convertible SUV filled with nude women and there were copious amounts of drug and alcohol. There were constant parties fueled by cocaine and sex, no rules and most importantly no police. It was a drug smuggler's paradise and Sodom and Gomorrah wrapped into one.

Carlos Lehder was an important player in the Medellin Cartel, instrumental to its immense wealth and influence. His role is so significant in fact that he is considered one of the Cartel's co-founders, along with Pablo and his brother Roberto.

Carlos life of crime started at his family's used car lot where he sold stolen American cars which he had smuggled into Columbia. He was a Nazi sympathizer and is said to have created a Neo-Nazi organization known as the National Latin Movement that ultimately sought to change the law regarding extradition of criminals to the United States. He also was a member of the paramilitary group MAS, which fought against the M-19 guerillas that would abduct members and family of the Cartel and hold them for ransom. The reason he joined was because he was abducted in 1981, but managed to escape sustaining just a bullet wound to the leg.

Carlos developed his highly evolved network of smuggling with the help of his cellmate George Jung, which was a veteran marijuana smuggler that used small planes flying at low altitudes to smuggle marijuana into the United States, this was adapted by Carlos and became the Cartel's modus operandi. Prior to Lehder's innovations regarding smuggling, cocaine would be brought to the States via human drug mules, which would either strap the drugs to their person or swallow them wrapped in condoms. An even risker tactic was smuggling the cocaine into the United States with other or enclosed in legal shipments, such as engine parts and industrial machinery. The second method though resulted in numerous seizures and losses of both profit and product. An interesting fact is that the first small plane Carlos and George used was actually stolen. Eventually due largely to Lehder's megalomaniacal tendencies he pushed Jung out of the partnership and continued smuggling independently. As proof of Lehder's unbelievable ego (and wealth), at the peak of his activity, when 300 kg of cocaine was being flown into the island daily, he offered to pay off Columbia's national debt to other countries in exchange for a free trade area where the Cartel could conduct its drug business unmolested. He attempted to buy off the entire Colombian government again in 1982 to avoid his extradition.

With the refinement of the smuggling process, the Cartel's financial power grew at an exponential rate.

During this point in time the total amount of cocaine being shipped to the United States by the Medellin Cartel monthly was a staggering 80 tons. It is said that the amounts where so immense that Lehder had used commercial jetliners at some point to move 22 tons of product.

Pablo's wealth was growing rapidly and he realized that he needed political power to ensure that he and his associates wouldn't be extradited to the United States and be convicted of their crimes. He started by buying or killing policemen, judges and public prosecutors. Plata o Plomo. Buying or killing off authorities wasn't enough to change the law regarding extradition though. Using his charisma and with immense investments in the poorer communities of Medellin, in the form of schools, football fields and housing for the poor, Pablo started developing a reputation as a champion of the poor. In some cases it is said that he would stand on a street corner in poor neighborhoods and giving money to people walking by. Because of this aforementioned community activity he was even well regarded by the Roman Catholic Church in Colombia. His grassroots campaign proved extremely effective and in 1982 he was voted into the Colombian Parliament as an alternative member. Before Pablo could take his position in the Parliament, a man that had made it his life's work to take down the Cartels, interment Minister of Justice at the time Rodrigo Lara, rejected Pablo as a murderous drug baron, presenting the media with evidence of his very first conviction (the 18kg of coca paste smuggling). After the media got ahold of the information regarding Pablo's criminal activity, Escobar was forced to leave the Parliament.

Although unknown to him at the time, this next action would be the first step towards the cliff that would bring his entire organization down. During a spring night as Minister Lara was driving home, two motorcycle flanked the minister's car and he was shot dead. The U.S. government being weary that an attempt against Minister Lara's life would be committed, issued him a bullet-proof vest, which he unfortunately wasn't wearing the night of the assassination. The minister's armed guard that was following in a Jeep pursued the gun men, apprehending one and killing the other. The twenty year old that committed the assassination revealed to authorities that he was paid $20,000 to kill the Minister. Pablo soon found out though that sometimes its better to deal with the devil you.

The War on Columbia

The man that replaced Rodrigo Lara, Enrique Parejo Gonzalez was a harsh and ruthless combatant of the Medellin Cartel. This was also the man that would sign Pablo Escobar's final arrest warrant.

The war waged against Pablo and the Cartel was an escalation though, of the three politician which made a hard push to extradite the narcotrafficantes; Luis Carlos Galan, Rodrigo Lara and Enrique Parejo Gonzalez, only Gonzalez survived. An attempt on his life was even made in 1987 as he served as Colombia's Ambassador to Hungary. He was given the post in Hungary under the fear that he would be assassinated in Colombia, unfortunately the Colombian Government underestimated Pablo's reach. On a cold morning Ambassador Gonzalez was walking to bus station when a man confronted him on the street, asked him his name, then shot him numerous times, one bullet going through his neck and lodging itself in Ambassador Gonzalez's spine.

Galan was a popular presidential candidate that was gunned down in Bogota as he spoke to a large group of people. As he spoke from a temporary stage in the rain, gunshots rang out through the crowd and the presidential candidate collapsed. The assassins had been hidden under the platform and shot through it, the bullets ripping through Galan, going under the bullet proof jacket he was wearing.

As a reaction to Minister Lara's assassination, the Colombian government immediately enacted extradition to United States, resulting in three of Pablo's close associates to be sent there and incarcerated.

It was during this period that Escobar revealed the true demon he was, with a terrorism campaign that would claim thousands more lives and haunt Colombia's collective consciousness for years to come.

The next period of Pablo's life would see the siege of the Colombian Supreme Court, the assassination of two more presidential candidates, the bombing of airliner and the leveling of a city block. This was a bloody period where terror reigned supreme over the innocent lives of Colombia.

In 1985 on the 6th of November, the M-19 guerilla group, speculated to be financed or commissioned by Pablo and the Cartel, mounted an attack on Colombia's Supreme Court. A squad of 35 guerilla soldiers entered the Palace of Justice via the basement. Upon exiting their vehicles they shot anyone in proximity indiscriminately. Moving through the building the guerilla forces took 300 hostages including many judiciary officials. As the siege and hostage situation bled into a second day, the state intervened with military force. The reason behind the attack is speculated to be because of Government of Colombia on the day of the siege was reviewing a constitutional law and entering a treating with the US, regarding extradition of narcotrafficantes and Cartel members. Ultimately, if this was in fact the motivation for the attack, it was successful, the treaty for U.S.-Colombian extradition treaty was voted down as unconstitutional a year later. This was just the first in a series of continually escalating terrorists attacks against the Colombia's Government and citizens.

The head of Colombia's equivalent of FBI, the Administrative Department of Security, General Miguel Maza became one of Escobar's most ardent pursuers. On the last day of May 1989, as General Maza and his security detail was driving through Bogota a bomb in a nearby car detonated, killing 4 people and injuring almost 40 others, amongst them school-children that were waiting for the bus.

Although the blast decimated the area and melted the wheels of the car Maza was in, he kicked open the door and walked away only with some lacerations.

Concurrently with these attacks and prosecutions by the Colombian Government the Medellin Cartel was also engaged in a brutal and bloody war with paramilitary groups funded by or backed by the Cali Cartel. Until this point Escobar, using the same methods of bribery, savagery, violence and intimidation had the majority of Colombian narcotrafficantes pay a 20-30% of their profits to him, uncontested. He had also set up an uneasy alliance with his main competitor the Cali Cartel, splitting distribution and entry points into the United States, with the Cali Cartel claiming New York, the Medellin Cartel claiming South Florida and Miami. Los Angeles was left unclaimed or up for grabs by either organization, although Escobar's associate Jose Gacha would eventually distribute to it via a smuggling route that ran through Mexico and

Texas. The Cali Cartel was formed by a group of Escobar's former associates and based in the Southern Colombian city of Cali.

As further testament to Escobar's ruthlessness, in an attempt to permanently silence presidential candidate and advocate for the extradition of narco-traffickers, Cesar Gaviria, he brought down a commercial flight killing over a hundred innocent people. No life had value for Escobar, not even the lives of the people that worked for him. The man that carried the bomb that brought down Avianca flight 203 was one of his own lieutenants that was told the suitcase he was carrying was a recording device. On November 27th 1989 a hillside became littered with the bodies of over one hundred people that where at the wrong place at the wrong time. The line between life and death in Colombia during this time was *that* finite. In seeming turn of cosmic justice, Gaviria wasn't even on the plane due to changes to his schedule. Gaviria would later go on to spearhead the creation of the Search Bloc, an elite group of drug enforcement police tasked with bringing Escobar to justice.

A little more than a week later on December 6, 1989, a school bus carrying half a metric ton of dynamite was detonated in the capital of Colombia, Bogota. The blast killed 70 innocent people and injured a staggering 1000, including women and children. The explosion was a second attempt against General Maza's life, but also had the ultimate goal of terrorizing the Colombian people, law enforcement and government. The blast was so intense that the chassis of the bus carrying the explosives was found on the 11th floor of the DAS (the Administrative Department of Security) building. These terrorist attacks not only intensified efforts to dismantle and destroy the Medellin Cartel and Pablo Escobar, but also cemented his status as a ruthless, murderous drug dealer to the public that had so readily embraced him previously.

This was followed in 1990 by a series of kidnappings of dignitaries and government officials. He intended on using the individuals kidnapped as collateral during negotiations preceding his surrender, or in the case that he was apprehended, the government officials would be used to levy his release. In retaliation for the newly formed Search Bloc and its destructive activity against Pablo and the Cartel's interest, Pablo put an indiscriminate bounty on all policemen. This resulted in a bloodbath that claimed 400 police officers' lives from 1992 to 1998, which even included police which weren't involved with the Search Bloc. Pablo paid street level thugs 3000 American dollars for each dead police officer.

The Search Bloc

Unbeknownst to Escobar all these previous bloody terrorist acts would set up the confluence of events that would lead to his own and the Cartel's demise. There were two American citizens killed on the Avianca Flight 203, allowing the United States to participate in the search for Pablo Escobar. They did so by offering technological/surveillance assistance and also helped in the training the newly formed Search Bloc. This group of incorruptible police officers, trained as elite soldiers where led by the irrepressible Colonel Hugo Martinez. The Search Bloc was essentially a highly trained Swat Team with hundreds of men and immense intelligence gathering capabilities. Colonel Martinez knew everything about Escobar by tapping practically every form of communication Pablo had available to him.

Colonel Martinez knew such mundane things about Escobar like his taste for silk sheets, his preference for white Nike shoes and what his favorite music. This intimacy of knowledge didn't go unrequited, after failing to bribe Martinez, the Cartel offered a cadet a "Plata o Plomo" deal to kill Colonel Martinez or be killed along with his family. According to Martinez the cadet had a change of heart as he had the gun turned on the Colonel and his finger on the trigger. They bribed a chef to poison the General's food and of course multiple bombings and drive by shootings, which were the Cartel's calling card. Through all this Colonel Martinez continued wagging war with the nefarious organization and their even more nefarious leader Pablo Escobar.

Escobar knew that he was being watched and under surveillance, in one case as Colonel Martinez listened in to one of Pablo's conversations he told Martinez, knowing he was listening, that he would not only kill him but also his family to the third degree, he would also exhume his grandparents put a bullet in their heads and then put them back in the ground. Escobar made multiple attempts to kill Martinez, but all them proved unsuccessful. Martinez retired in city of Bogota, whereas we all know how Pablo's life ended.

La Catedral

After this sequence of vicious terrorist attacks Pablo entered into an uneasy truce with the Colombian Government to turn himself in. Some reference the death of his close associate, right hand man, confidante and some say brains behind the Medellin Cartel, cousin Gustavo Gaviria, by Search Bloc as a huge motivation for Pablo's surrender. Another reason Pablo agreed to turn himself in was that the Supreme Court had thrown out the extradition treaty Colombia was considering entering with the United States since 1989 (around the time of Palace of Justice siege which the consideration of the treaty was speculated to be the motivation behind the attack). The agreement also included that Escobar would only serve a maximum prison term of five years.

Much like Escobar's other agreements though, this one with the Colombian government would be executed on his terms.

A special prison was built, to Escobar's specifications, *with* government funds on a hillside overlooking his hometown of Medellin. The agreement included that the prison's security staff would be chosen by Escobar for fear that his enemies would make attempts against his life, using guards. La Catedral was built essentially as a fortress, to protect Escobar than to incarcerate him. The prison's facilities included amenities such as a football pitch, a hot tub, a computer (which was a rarity) and cellphones (which were even more of a rarity). It is said that he even requested a telescope looking towards his daughter's house so he could see her when they spoke on the telephone. Escobar could come and go as he wished and continued serving as the head of Medellin Cartel, while within the prison. To the point that he would have meetings with the "capos" (lieutenants) of the organizations within the walls of the prison.

This wasn't a secret either, locals and authorities would mockingly call the prison "Hotel Escobar" or "Club Medellin".

Another speculation as to why Escobar turned himself in was that he had a huge target on his back at the time. The Medellin cartel was not only at war with the Cali Cartel at the time, it was also at war with the paramilitary groups funded by the Cali Cartel. A group known as Los Pepes funded by the Cali Cartel, used the Cartel's same brutal tactics of torture, intimidation and murder, to kill 300 of Escobar's closest associates and even family members. Concurrently with this perfect storm, the Search Bloc (aforementioned in previous chapter) headed by the incorruptible, one-minded and extremely motivated Colonel Hugo Martinez was heatedly pursuing Escobar. Pablo's rein was coming to a violent and bloody end.

Los Pepes

Pablo was trying to protect and sustain his organization, while fighting on multiple front. This war was happening all over the Americas not just in Escobar's native Colombia. In the U.S. the DEA continued seizing any cocaine shipments they discovered and helped the Colombian police in their missions mounted against the Cartel. In fact the destruction of one the Cartel's largest jungle coca paste processing lab, La Tranquilandia was a joint Colombian Police-DEA mission. In Colombia, Escobar and the Cartel was being threatened by multiple enemies, including their rival the Cali Cartel and various paramilitary groups funded by them. Although the Search Bloc and Colonel Martinez proved to be a formidable adversary, killing co-founder of the Cartel, Jose Gacha "The Mexican" and the Cartel's 8th capo in command

Gilberto Rendon, there was an enemy that was much more damaging.

Known as Los Pepes, a paramilitary group funded by the Cali Cartel, implemented the same brutal tactics as the Medellin Cartel, to devastating effect. The Los Pepes name roughly translates to "The Prosecuted by Pablo Escobar". Los Pepes claimed to be comprised of victims of Pablo Escobar, but in fact one of their founders was a close associate to Pablo, working with him to fund his previous paramilitary group Los Tangueros. But Pablo's greed and ruthlessness made an enemy that would cut through his organization like a flaming sword. After trying to kill the founder of the Los Pepes, Fidel Castano in La Catedral, Fidel vowed revenge, brutal, bloody and ruthless revenge.

They would beginning a campaign of murder, picking off a slew of Escobar's collaborators, leaving them in plain view and hanging a sign off the cadavers' neck that read (in rough translation) "For working with Pablo Escobar the narcoterrorista and baby killer – Los Pepes". They incinerated the government building that held all of Escobar's luxury automobiles, which was assumed would be returned to the drug lord after he was released. Eventually their systematic murder of anyone associated with Escobar, forced many of Escobar's associates to surrender. It was speculated that members of the Search Bloc, where pulling double duty as members of the Los Pepes' death squads.

By the end of Los Pepes' one year war with Pablo Escobar and his Cartel, they had left the Cartel decimated, and Escobar fearing for the safety of his family. They had managed to shake the drug baron like no other organization that had mounted a campaign against him had. People that had witnessed the carnage said that if Escobar used a car bomb against the people of Colombia the Los Pepes would detonated three against Pablo's interest.

An interesting conspiracy theory speculates that the Los Pepes were not only funded by Escobar's main competitors, the Cali Cartel, shared members with the Search Bloc, but was also created by the CIA to combat Escobar and the Medellin Cartel with the same brutal methods they used themselves. The involvement of the United States government in the war against the Cartel wasn't classified but this would take America's involvement to a different level being behind a what was essentially a death-squad. No matter what the truth, the multiple fronts Escobar was being fought on sent the Cartel into a nose-dive it would never be able to recover from.

The Fall Of An Empire

The mounting pressure on Escobar would be the reason he went to El Catedral but his hubris would soon catch up to him. While in the prison Escobar ordered two street level members of the Cartel to be tortured and killed at El Catedral. Eventually this event was exposed to the great embarrassment of the Colombian government. The reaction was swift and determined, if poorly executed. The Colombian Government and Judicial system decided to transfer Escobar from his luxurious faux prison to a real prison to serve the remainder of his prison term, which was still four years. Initially two officials, Eduardo Mendoza which was the interment Deputy Justice Minister and Lieutenant Colonel Hernando Navas, visited El Catedral to inform Pablo of his impending transfer. This infuriated Escobar and his associates, so the two government officials were taken hostage at the prison.

The Colombian Police converged on El Catedral, killing several of Pablo's guards and associates and saving the two officials. Yet Escobar still managed to make a slick escape unscathed according to some just by walking out the back door of the prison as a hail of bullets rained on the front. After his escape Pablo went immediately into hiding. Escobar was on the lam for over a year, bouncing from safe house to safe house. As Pablo ran, the Los Pepes continued killing off his associate. In a strange twist of irony Pablo was also killing his fair share of associates. This was because the U.S. intelligence gathering service (codename Centra Spike) that was helping Colombian authorities, had become so effective at surveying Escobar, that he started to think he had a traitor in his midst. Pablo, was becoming increasingly paranoid torturing and killing the few associates he had left.

During this time Pablo also tried to get his family out of Colombia for fear that the Los Pepes would eventually turn on them. They attempted to travel to Germany but were turned away, the Columbian authorities escorted the Escobar family to hotel which was said to be owned by the Columbian Justice Department. Under police protection and surveillance, the family remained there, while the man hunt for patriarch Pablo continued.

Previous to this though Pablo completely fell off the face of the Earth. For months Centra Spike, The Search Bloc and Colombian law enforcement scoured the airwaves, streets and Pablo's old haunts, looking for any evidence that could lead them to Escobar. The Cartel now being leaderless, shaken to its core and weakened by the wave of the Los Pepes killings, was looking for leadership, unfortunately Pablo was in hiding and unable to fulfill this role. The responsibility fell to Juan Pablo, Escobar's son which became his impromptu point man and communication bridge between the drug lord and the cartel. Juan Pablo was in frequent communication with his father conveying his orders and commands to the Cartel's men.

During one of their increasingly frequent telephone conversations with his son, the Colombian authorities managed to triangulate and find Pablo's location. They followed the signal to a upper middle class neighborhood of Los Olivos. The person that was at the lead of the search was in fact commander of the Search Bloc Colonel Martinez's son, Hugo Martinez. Although an extremely competent policeman and leader, Hugo's first triangulation was incorrect, due to a small body of water running next to hideout which deflected the radio signals and gave a false result. The police raided this building as Pablo continued his conversation. Hugo Martinez adjusted his instruments and drove by a house trying to re-triangulate as he closed in on the actual position, he saw the undeniable silhouette of Pablo Escobar, still talking on the telephone with Juan Pablo. Due to the multiple sacrifices, the persistence and unparalleled bravery of the men of the Search Bloc, Colombian Justice Department and Colombian Police, the 15 month manhunt had come to a culmination. Ironically Pablo's end would come just one day after his birthday. With Brigadier Hugo Martinez at the helm of the operation, he informed his father General Martinez that they had a positive ID on Escobar. Although his father said that the team should wait for reinforcements, he said that apprehending Pablo was of the utmost importance. According to Martinez, their eyes met as he made a second pass by the two story house in Los Olivos. Brigadier Martinez's team converged on the house Pablo was holed up in.

The team breached the door with an explosive charge and the team entered the building. Until this point Pablo was completely unaware of the operation. Brigadier Martinez, moved up to the second floor of the hideout. A lone bodyguard, El Limon, was shot as he attempted to escape,

Escobar fled on the adjacent rooftops through a window, looking for a avenue of escape. Initially Pablo found cover behind the low jagged walls of the houses that bordered the roof he was on, but as he moved along the roofs he came out of cover.

He was shot in the leg, in the torso and the fatal blow, a shot in the right ear.

General Martinez's son came over the radio and was heard saying (in rough translation) "Viva (long live) Colombia, Escobar is dead". Everyone involved jubilated at the sound of this victorious phrase. The bloody, murderous era of Escobar's narcoterrorism was finally over.

There is an interesting theory revolving around the shot that killed Pablo. The shot that entered Pablo's right ear, many speculate was a coup de grace, administered by one of his rooftop pursuers. These men had seen many of their comrades die at the hands of the Medellin Cartel and under Pablo's orders, so he was given no quarter.

Another theory postulated by his son, said that Pablo probably killed himself to avoid being tortured as an act of revenge. A third theory says that there is a legend going around the Delta Force community, that a Delta Force sniper had administered the death shot from an unbelievable distance. Even though Delta Force wasn't officially involved multiple eye-witness reports and anonymous sources say that indeed elite Delta Force special operations personnel contributed to the efforts to apprehend Escobar.

Plomo por Pablo

As Pablo Escobar laid dead on the rooftop, Colombian National Police members posed over him with rifles, the DEA agent Steve Murphy that had spent years pursuing Escobar, squatted over Escobar's body and was also photographed. Although it was a resounding success and a serious hit to the cocaine trade, Pablo's voice would echo on for years to come. His murderous rein, enforced by death, torture and intimidation would leave a scar on the mentality of the Colombian people, some argue forever. Almost every single innocent Colombian citizen had been touched by the death that Pablo so readily spread.

Although The Medellin Cartel's infamous founder and ruthless leader was dead, cocaine trafficking still remained alive and well, if not fragmented. Medellin remained the capital of coca paste processing and smuggling, the Cali Cartel taking over the majority of the trade and filling the power vacuum the death of Escobar created. Two years later though, the Cali Cartel was also dismantled with the capture of two of its leaders, the Rodriguez brothers. This created an holistic fragmentation which saw the rise of multiple so-called "Baby Cartel", paramilitary groups and organizations founded by former Cali and Medellin Cartel members. It is even said that the Los Pepes that had previously stood as anti-narcos terrorist, became narcos themselves.

Of course these factions, groups and paramilitary organizations were constantly locked in bloody turf wars, for years after the death of Escobar. Since Pablo's death, no single figure-head has been seen leading a trafficking ring to the scale that Escobar did. This is because of the fragmented nature of the cocaine trade and the fact that both Colombian authorities and DEA make sure that any criminal that manages to ascend through the ranks is quickly dealt with.

The only true contemporary approximation to Pablo's success is the Mexican drug baron Joaquin Guzman "El Chapo" which is one of the heads of the Sinaloa Cartel, that is more a conglomerate than a singular Cartel with one leader. Currently Guzman is incarcerated in the United States, after multiple successful escapes.

Although this fragmentation might seem like a positive effect, unfortunately the opposite is true. The latest iteration of the drug cartel known as BARCRIMs (abbreviation for bandas criminales or band of criminals) are so loosely organized that they are almost impossible to dismantle. Few have defined leadership, they are organized into smaller independent groups that defend their turf with bloody effectiveness. The most well known are the *Urabenos, Oficina de Envigado* and *Rastrojos.*

Making matters worse for authorities is the fact that many of the new Cartels or drug trafficking cells, subcontract violence to other criminal gangs and seldom engage in violent activity and heavily implement new technology to facilitate their activities. Some Mexican Cartels have even used drones to smuggle shipments of cocaine over international borders, between Mexico and the United States.

Escobar left a bloody swath in the history of Colombia, killing innocent people indiscriminately. His wealth and surreally luxurious lifestyle has recently been sensationalized and glorified, but the reality of Escobar's life can be contextualized in the fact that he died barefoot on the rooftop, running away from law enforcement like a common street thug. People like President Gaviria and General Martinez which risked their life every day they dedicated to bringing Escobar to justice should be glorified. People like Presidential candidate Luis

Galan which lost their life for no other reason than trying to quell a murderous greedy drug lord.

He left his home country in disarray, the only thing that his children and widow inherited was the weight of the murders that their father committed. His son Juan Pablo Escobar was even forced to change his name, ashamed of the legacy of death his father bestowed on the name "Escobar". He tried to live a normal life as Juan Sebastian Marroquin Santos an Argentinian architect. Eventually the burden of his father's victims and their relatives was too much for Juan Sebastian and in 2009 he went public both his identity and with an apology. In the documentary titled *Sins of My Father* he apologized to Escobar's victims, the Colombian people and the world. The documentary was made in collaboration with Escobar's wife that is Juan's mother and two victims of his father's violence.

In an ironic twist, the one thing that Pablo valued more than his drug empire and money was his family, which he cursed with his legacy of violence. Not only was he unable to leave any of his 25 billion dollar fortune, he cursed them to live in complete obscurity, bouncing from one country to another each time their identities where revealed. Even his daughter which was his favorite, according to his associates, "Pablo's spoiled princess". Some stories say that when the family was on the run, towards the end of Escobar's life, had burned two million dollars when Manuela complained she was cold. Little is know about Escobar's little princess other than she has been moving since her father's death.

Outro

Although most Colombians would reel at the mere mention of the Escobar name, there are still areas, especially the poor areas of Medellin, where Pablo is still extoled as a hero. Mural juxtapose Pablo's visage with an image of Jesus. Escobar won favor by building housing, football pitches and actually giving out money on street corners. His ultimately goal though was to create a human shield out of these unassuming and desperately impoverished communities.

Some Colombians even celebrate the anniversary of his death like other countries celebrate national heroes. Unfortunately he is celebrated more in the media. Innumerous documentaries, dramatized series and books exist, describing the life and times of the real life Tony Montana. Granted his unbelievable wealth, gained through ruthless tactics and selling powdered death is undeniably an intriguing narrative, the reality of his actions amount to very little more than greed and murder.

Much like Tony Montana the world was his for only a moment.

The gap that Pablo left in the international drug trade created an seemingly invincible multi-headed Hydra. Today the cocaine trade still continues to claim hundreds of thousands of lives, gangs fighting over turf, people being murdered and robbed to secure a gram or two of crack cocaine and the innocent people that happened to find themselves in the deadly cross-fire.

Although Medellin and Colombia at large held the dishonorable title of murder capital of the world, places like Juarez, Mexico, Caracas, Venezuela, San Pedro, Honduras and San Salvador, El Salvador came to fill in the bloody gap. Most of these places, worked with Pablo during his rein, distributing his murderous wares or sourcing the raw material. Once Escobar was out of the picture and his control weaned, these places broke out on their own. They honored Escobar's legacy though, spreading his favorite product along with the murder its. demands because of the greed it creates. His narcoterrorist successors in fact made murder and violence a closer bedmate than the Medellin Cartel ever did.

One of the biggest drug cartels at the moment the Sinaloa Cartel, made infamous not only because of their slippery leader Joaquin "El Chapo" (the dude or the Lil' Dude) Guzman, but also because of their murderous ways. The Sinaloa cartel developed its reputation not only because its leader is a cocaine dealing Houdini approximation, but because they spread their reign with murder and violence. They have killed bus loads of civilians for refusing to work with them, on a stretch of road that has come to be known as the "Murder Highway". Few travel this road and those that do, are heavily arm and drive at high speeds. This road is perpetually littered with bullet riddled burnt cars and decapitated bodies.

The Los Zetas Cartel, initially founded by special forces soldiers that deserted, threw two grenades into a group of 30,000 people, celebrating Mexico's independence day. The attacked killed several people and injured hundreds.

This is the legacy Escobar left the world, death motivated by greed. If you purchased this book expecting a story of a poor boy from a working class family that became one of the world's wealthiest individuals by the time he was in his mid-thirties, then I apologize. The reality of Pablo was a dark one, one mired in the blood of innocent people, death on the altar of greed and that ultimately ended with a coward's death running from true heroes. He has become a faux-celebrity and admired within circles that revere primal and fake bravado, a bravado built on innocent victims and on the backs of the people that stand next to them. When everything is stripped away though, they are nothing more than a barefoot criminal, fallen by the bullets of real heroes.

Printed in Great Britain
by Amazon

27191013R00036